More Advance Praise for a half-red sea

"Evie Shockley gives us, beautifully, the sound of justice, the voice of *aware* (Afro) America, and the soul music of consciousness. In these unapologetically excellent, astonishingly sensual, whimsically political, and fiercely personal poems, Shockley uses the moral clarity of history to reveal how foolish we become when we forget our roots. Herein Phillis Wheatley seems to upbraid Condoleeza Rice, while Harriet Tubman upholds Anita Hill. The poet herself forges culture out of pop culture and a family out of diaspora. You may hear, in the margins here, a touch of Robert Hayden and Ishmael Reed, a lick of Lucille Clifton and Ntozake Shange. That's just homage: Shockley be an awesome power in her own right. Read these poems and go, 'Damn!'"
—**GEORGE ELLIOTT CLARKE**

"Evie Shockley isn't waiting for the waters to part; her words work their own miracles. Read them and feel free. Read them, too, and beware: the world is wicked. As the poet says, evil is clever. But Evie is more clever. The very forms of her poems are a whack back at fate. Their sounds unshackle us. Egypt to the right, Cannan ahead—each line speaks a bridge into being." —**JOSEPH DONAHUE**

"Evie Shockley's poetry is a vortex, a delta where a hundred streams meet and deposit their rich traffic. In one poem she channels the past, relaying conversations between ancestral women; in another she telegraphs the future, holding a thousand words in a single tortured frame. Shockley is a single voice and a whole choir; now she speaks, now she sings, now she writes; all the while she signifies and she languages. Readers of *a half-red sea* will find a history of African-American writing and witness as well as a set of new experimental paths—call them trials of the poem—along which the next steps are being taken, just now." —**DAVID KELLOGG**

a half-red sea

Evie Shockley

Poetry Series #10

CAROLINA WREN PRESS
Durham, North Carolina

The mission of Carolina Wren Press is to seek out, nurture and promote literary work by new and underrepresented writers, including women and writers of color.

Editor: David Kellogg

Design: Lesley Landis Designs
Cover Image: "Red Sea" © 2004 Maria Entis

This publication was made possible in part by generous grants from the North Carolina Arts Council. In addition, we gratefully acknowledge the ongoing support made possible through gifts to the Durham Arts Council's United Arts Fund.

Library of Congress Cataloguing-in-Publication Data:

Shockley, Evie, 1965-
A half-red sea : poems / Evie Shockley.
p. cm. -- (Carolina Wren Press poetry series ; 10)
ISBN 0-932112-53-6
1. African Americans—Poetry. I. Title. II. Series.

PS3619.H63H35 2006
811'.6--dc22

2006017138

for my mother and father, who love
even when they cannot approve

and for Stéphane,
who proves love's brave

"You propose my returning to Africa with Bristol Yamma and John Quamine…? Upon my arrival, how like a Barbarian shou'd I look to the Natives; I can promise that my tongue shall be quiet/for a strong reason indeed/being an utter stranger to the language of Anamaboe."

—*Letter from Phillis Wheatley to John Thornton, October 30, 1774*

if the seas of cities
should crash against each other
and break the chains
and break the walls holding down the cargo
and break the sides of the seas
and all the waters of the earth wash together
in a rush of breaking
where will the captains run and
to what harbor?

—*Lucille Clifton*

contents

i. passage

ii. rafts

iii. pull

i. passage

possibilities of poetry, upon her death

ars poetica, rough ship, drag
        me from world to brutal word,
                mental passage. (write.) be
a wail of a sound, surfacing
        to fountain dark water found
                in valleys of shadow of breath.
i will brook no evil, for
        thou art not gone, gwen,
                and poems made of tears
evaporate. when the drops
        dry, scrape gray lines of salt
                and dreams from brown faces.
(rite.) melt like a verb into
        this rich white earth of paper.
                grow an oeuvre from a need.

for gwendolyn brooks (1917–2000)

london bridge

deep river   my home is over jordan
entering the cathedral i hear these (re)moving words
echoing off the tear-stained glass windows
people from a hundred nations   wet with london

rain   dripping from their hair and umbrellas   pooling
into puddles   the spit of fifty foreign tongues
visa'd by christ   the choir mouths open   a blues
estuary   stems the vernacular tide   de-negros de notes
refrains from a spiritual funk   imports

my pass(ed)   re-fines the raw product   the no of my
yesterday   onyx pearls   lost overboard   what the

hell could not hold   so many   in the same boat
othello came to england during elizabeth's reign
moored to the stage   the noblest of savages   he
entertained the idea of robeson   st. paul's

immaculate reception   the thames not an ole man to
sing home about   but on its shores the solid

opulence of the anglican church   a veritable
vault of safety from enemy bombs   starvation   sale
excommunication the greatest threat   not to be
refused the shelter of its thick stone walls

just swallow this wafer of state and be swallowed
open your heart to the god of gladstone dis-
raeli and churchill   must jesus bear this cross alone
devil on the deep blue sea   just one more bon voyage
across the atlantic   the pacific   the world awaits   you'd
not have thought death had unhomed so many

bio / autography
(or, 18th-century multiculturalism)

found in africa / *dawned in freedom*
raised in boston / *rose in slavery*
schooled in greek / *grew in god*
published in england / *died in poverty*

                        for phillis wheatley

pantoum: landing, 1976

dreaming the lives of the ancestors,
you awake, justly terrified of this world:
you could dance underwater and not get wet,
you hear, but the pressure is drowning you:

you're awake, but just terrified of this world,
where all solids are ice: *underwater boogie,*
you hear, but the press sure is drowning you:
the igbo were walking, not dancing:

where all solids are ice, *underwater boogie*
is good advice, because they're quick to melt:
the igbo were straight up walking, not dancing:
and you've still got to get through this life:

take my advice, quickly: they're melting:
you could dance underwater and not get wet:
and you've got to, to get through this life still
dreaming the lives of the ancestors

waiting on the mayflower

> *"what, to the american slave, is your 4th of july?"*
> *—frederick douglass*

i. august 1619

arrived in a boat. named
and unnamed. twenty, pirated

away from a portuguese
slaver. traded for victuals.

drowned in this land of fresh,
volatile clearings and folk

with skin like melted
cowrie shells. soon shedding

servitude. soon reaping
talents sown on african soil.

after indenture, christians,
colonists. not english, but

not yet not-white. antoney
and isabella, whose marriage

stretched the short shadows
of america's early afternoon

into the dusky reaches of evening,
whose conjugal coitus spent

first the choice coin of africa
on rough virginian citizenship,

baptized their son, william,
into the church of england.

ii. december 1638

fear must have shuddered
into boston on the backs

of true believers—men and
women of an unadorned god—

deep in the heavy black fabric
of their coats and dresses like

a stench. black a mark of
pride they wore as if branded,

never dreaming they could
take it off. envy anticipated

their advent. glittered at them,
settling in, from the knife

blades of the massachusetts.
seeped like low-pitched

humming from the fur
lining the natives' warm

blankets. but *desire* docked
in 1638. in from the harbor

flocked a people whose eyes
sparked like stars, even near

death. whose hair promised
a mixture of cotton and river

water and vines, a texture
the fingers ached for. who

wholly inhabited a skin the
midnight color of grace

that clarified the hue of the
pilgrims' woolen weeds. fear

and envy claimed pride of place,
put *desire's* cargo to good use.

iii. march 1770

that night, crispus attucks
dreamed. how he'd attacked

his would-be master and fled
in wild-eyed search of self-

determination. discarded
virginia on the run and ran

out of breath in salt-scented
boston. found there, if not

freedom, fearlessness. a belief
in himself that rocked things

with the uncontrolled power
of the muscular atlantic, power

to cradle, to capsize. awoke
angry again at the planter

who'd taken him for a mule
or a machine. had shouldered

a chip the size of concord
by the time the redcoat dared

to dare him. died wishing he'd
amassed such revolutionary

ire in virginia. died dreaming
great britain was the enemy.

*iv. july 4th: last
     but not least*

17-, 18-, 19-76 and still
this celebration's shamed

with gunpowder and words
that lie like martyrs in cold

blood. africa's descendents,
planting here year after year

the seeds of labor, sweating
bullets in this nation's wars,

have harvested the rope,
the rape, the ghetto, the cell,

the fire, the flood, and the
blame for you-name-it. so

today black folks barbeque
ribs and smother the echoes

of billie's strange song in
sauces. drink gin. gladly

holiday to heckle speeches
on tv. pretend to parade.

turn out in droves for distant
detonations, chaos, controlled

as always, but directed
away from us tonight. stare

into the mirror of the sky
at our growing reflection,

boggled by how america
gawks at the passing pinpoints

of flame, but overlooks the vast,
ebony palm giving them shape.

o pioneer!

"and the lord said unto satan, behold, he is in
thine hand; but save his life." —job 2:6

he made history sit up stiff like a new recruit waiting wide-eyed

for the next gust from winds of change. did another job

on the devil, in tailored sackcloth, catered ashes. sometimes he hears

the children's voices louden slightly, as if they were coming back.

they are not. he claps his hands when no one's looking, in time

with their dancing footsteps' receding: a memory, a summons

ignored. all up in the sun's face, his melanin bubbles to the surface

like struck oil. he snaps his past around him, a matador's cape, to keep

himself from disappearing, becoming some black hole consumed

with its own success. he is a brewing storm, high but heavy, hanging

like a veil over that yellow daystar until he bursts into spears.

for craig griffith, byron taylor, and stanley stallworth

not in the causal chain

i you she liu they shiites we mericans girls he williams coloreds you

heartbreak loss ignorance fear rage grief desire pride greed despair

redwood him appeal fans family limb mobility savings clique her faith

might *possibly* *ought* *theoretically* **could** *probably* *would* *maybe* *should*

fire hurricane knife needle law penis gun wage tornado tongue wish

lung brain kidney seed motor mind tide memory evolution soul heart

end pass stop decease terminate stop cease transition fail stop quit **die**

castillo del morro: calling your bluff
　　　—san juan, puerto rico

three slits of windows
look out from the look-
out posts   guard   the out-

look's blue   three hundred
degrees   light years   spot
the threat   wait to see

the whites of their lies
shoot   safety made of brick
mortar   concrete   sheeting

thick walls   cannons   can-
nonballs   bars of iron
boulders   rocks   rough

muscular winds   ocean's
pulsing thrusts   rampant
ramparts   offensive

defense   elementally
exposed parapets
always something wet

something thundering
gusts against ears blow
beating irises

to blue pools   trenches
sluice waste fluids to
outlets   bloodletting

pores sweating   forget
it   getting fortrest
is just too damn hard

art of dakar (or, tourist trap)

> *"a senegalese activist reported that trees, some more than a century old,*
> *had been cut down everywhere the [u.s.] president was scheduled to pass."*
> —*jonah engle,* the nation, *7/23/2003*

poems are bullshit unless they are trees a century old, sentries lining the streets of senegal. in dakar, the darker brother keeps his peace, while a bush burns in effigy. a poem should show, not tell, so hold up your arms as if they were trees: if you have enough digits to make a fist, you are now a double amputee. terror perches in branches with its sights set on power ties, so no trees on these roots. a poem in jeopardy appeals perversely to the senses. the space where what you haven't seen used to be *(what did these trees look like?).* less traffic on the main thoroughfares *(what did these trees smell like?).* using *like* or *as,* describe the impact of the visit on the city: dakar, comatose quadriplegic, stunned by the thundering walk and big stick of a blowhard. and where are the residents of gorée island, while the resident of a white house tours a red one? come on, concentrate. clean shot photo ops, souvenirs at low low prices. all sales final: no return.

atlantis made easy

orange was the color of her address, then blue silt : : whiskey burned brown down the
street, then a dangerous drink whirled around a paper umbrella : : intoxication blue
across the porch then rose in the attic : : bloated tuesday taught us, she's never been dry
and never will be : : brass, bass, ivory, skins : : i hate to see that ninth ward wall go
down : : army corpse engineers ran a 'train on her : : aw chere : : sweet ghost, saturated,
deserted : : teething ground for the expected spectre, we knew it'd show up better late
(against a black backdrop), whenever : : wait in the water, wait in the water, children : :
stub your soul on a granite memory, a marble key change, an indigo mood : : trouble
(the water)

cause i'm from dixie too

i am southern hear me roar i am burning flags bearing crosses i am scarlett and prissy like a piece of carmine velvet at christmas don't know nothing bout birthin no rabies so don't come foamin at my mouth i am miss dixie and a miss is as good as a guile i am a daughter of the con-federacy come on dad don't you know me here let me put on this hood and sheet do my eyes look more familiar now surrounded by bleach i am southern damn it y'all keep forgetting my birth was our wedding till death do us part i took the gal out of tennessee but the south came back to me the north left me cold though there's southern heat i could do without i.e. stick to barbequing cows and pigs but i'll take a late summer and a fall so long i land right back in piedmont eden hell it's hot i am southern got this drawl that comes from s-wallowing final consonants cuss words loose meaning gonna spew it all back at you sew it in ink on the fabric of a myth of a land of cotton on page after rotten page book away book away book away dixie-banned o swee-tea honey sugar dumpling pie i'll swallow more so much sweet stuff my magnolias will shoot out blossoms protruding raw cane this is my legacy the freak will inherit the mirth aw aw aw mammy don't you want me don't you want me home come on mammy i mean miss anne i may be your ugly duckling now but those folk up north will see me no more when i get to that swan-y shore

the last temptation: a 21st-century bop odyssey

there were many thousands of black people—
enough to fill a football stadium—all shuffling
side to side in time to marley's *exodus,* gathered
to celebrate the irrelevance of blackness. *who
needs it?* the posters proudly proclaimed
in big black—i mean, block—letters.

*it was just my imagination
running away with me*

with me and ellison's invisible man, briefcases
still heavily in hand. why not just burn the papers,
drop the shades, dump the cast-iron smiles
into the trash, and flush the now-empty bags
down the sewer? we had nothing to lose
but our balance—nothing to risk but tripping
over the castaways later on. baggage free
at last, he gave me some skin. was it black?
i had nowhere to put it, so i gave it back.

*but it was just my imagination   once again
running away with me*

with me and harriet t. maybe she can't
turn her staff into a snake, but she can turn
a backwards-looking negro into a free
black, using nothing but a pistol
and a dead-on sense of direction. hey,
there she is! and look where she's headed—

*it   was   just my imagination
running*

unbelievable sale!

as advertised on travelprofity.com:

martin luther king, jr. day
getaways!

need a tan? try our white flights!
ride first-class on a one-way ticket out
of the city! you won't touch ground
until you've left the trash and crime
behind you...

or go for our premiere package—
a round-trip ticket whisks you off
to the suburbs and luxurious
ranch-style accommodations! stay
as long as you want—you
or your children
may take advantage of the return flight
whenever property values drop
to the right price for you!

too much sun? customers
with a natural tan should try
our equal opportunity special—passage
on our cross-country subway
to the northern destination of your
choice! avoid the struggles and harassments
of above-ground travel!

(subway fares subject to increase without
notice. taxes, at the rate of 3/5ths of
the value of the passenger, not included
in the price of the ticket.)

or may we interest you in our
trans-atlantic cruise...?

elocation (or, exit us)

        the city is american, so she
can map it. train tracks, highways slice through, bleed
        only to one side. like a half-red sea
permanently parted, the middle she'd

        pass through, like the rest, in a wheeling rush,
afraid the divide would not hold and all
        would drown—city as almighty ambush—
beneath the crashing waves of human hell.

        the city's infra(red)structure sweats her,
a land(e)scape she can't make, though she knows
        the way. she's got great heart, but that gets her
where? egypt's always on her right (it goes

        where she goes), canaan's always just a-head,
and to her left, land of the bloodless dead.

a thousand words

ii. rafts

wheatley and hemmings have drinks
in the halls of the ancestors

cheers! they clink and each one
                knocks one back, rockless scotch
whiskey. phillis is unfazed, despite

                her slight frame: holds her liquor
like she holds her tongue. sally's
                less circumspect, hums along

with her buzz. those two've been
                doing drinks since mark twain
was in diapers. staked out a table

                overlooking sally's descendents,
whose affairs keep them beaming
                and cackling. phillis scratches

lines on a napkin. they both like
                young twain's book about a boy
and a man on a raft, encourage

                sally's kin to read it. *everything*
moves along, long as they stay on
                the river, sally says, as though

the living hear her. newcomers ask
                about the stately older woman
with a parisian lilt coasting on her

                uneducated english tête-à-tête
with that thin young chick who
                looks and snaps like a whip.

the bartender wipes his counter,
        keeps his counsel. now and then
someone will overhear their names,

        know just enough to be curious
and not enough to leave the two
        alone. approaching the table,

the someone gushes: *i have to know—*
        was it love? for you and thomas? or
you? susanna? dark and light eyes

        look into each other, then turn
on the interrogator, untamed.
        what kind of question is that? one

of them asks. *tell me. what kind?*
        after someone backs away, sally
always says, *you ain't got to be*

        smart to be among the ancestors. no,
phillis shoots back, *just dead.* in
        silence they think on rivers and

rafts, then order another round.

you can say that again, billie

southern women serve strife   keep lines of pride open
trees are not taller than these broad vessels   femmes who
bear fully armored knights   clinking from the womb   but
a night in whining ardor   means black woman compelled   how
strange   brown vassal on a bed of green needles   ingests the
fruit of georgia   let that gestate   but be-gets no child of the south

blood tells the story   do you salute old gory   were you born
on a white horse or a black ass   everything depends upon
the way your rusty lifeflow writes   sutpenmanship   if it
leaves blond scribbled across your scalp   hurray
and blue inscribed in your eyes   praise the cause   your literary
blood wins the gene pool   it's a prize   hide your mama   baby
at worst you're a breast-seller   compelling octorune   but
the best cellars are dark and earthy   humid places where fears take
root   and grow up to be cowboys   yee-haw

the ballad of anita hill

i.

beside a graveled path, stately trees
        sweep back into a sudden arc: sun
cuts the bristly green rug. joggers wheeze
        to a walk, watch the quiet field become

a trembling of squirrels and small
        birds. cobwebs, dusty with dew,
cloud the shrubs: spiders enthrall,
        simply by spinning out silken sinews

fraught deep within them. bereft of fear,
        you were bright when you took center
stage: not dancing, perhaps, but clear:
        prickly with bloodless truths. winter

fell, heavy and wet, quite out of season,
        innocent. as if snow needs a reason.

ii.

sit up straight. smile. don't smile. wear
        that nice suit, you know, the blue one
with the knee-length hem. say a prayer:
        just a quick, silent "thy will be done."

bring your family (nuclear only). make
        sure they dress middle-class and hug
you affectionately. be strong, or fake
        it, but in a womanly way. don't be smug

or shy or prudish or loose, when testifying
        that he said "pussy" or "penis" on the job:
push the words out, as if they were defying
        gravity, then let them fly. weep. don't sob.

exude celibacy—heterosexual style.
    sit up straight. smile. don't smile.

iii.

we crowned you for a day, a week, miss black
    america: knew you as a round, brown face
pegged in a sharp, square frame: condemned your lack
    of style—those tailored suits could never grace

the breasts of chocolate milk, the fleshy hips
    we knew you had, the way an evening gown
would have: judged you on the size of your lips,
    their color, whether they trembled, or turned down:

considered your talents—writing, teaching law—
    yet ranked you highest for your undemonstrated
but patent skill at giving head (we saw
    through your disguise): and ultimately rated

you a queen-bitch-jezebel-matriarch-whore,
    destroyer of black manhood, and so much more.

protect yourself

a wall of stone   a fort of knocks
          a pain of glass   a heart of would
     a glass of wine   a love of less
a screen of smoke   a drink of drown   a light of day
     a dark of night   a close of mind
a shade of skin   a veil of hair   a suit of clothes
     a code of crack   a style of dress   a coat of paint
          a drug of choice   a pen of ink
a work of art   a word of praise
          a pass of word   a shield of sword
a voice of doom   a gun of shot   a kiss of death
     a foot of down   a arm of me   a war of sex
          a deaf of ear   a line of fire
a sea of blood   a eye of steel   a shore of line
     a look of hate   a fence of goods   a own of ship
     a lock of box   a wad of cash   a band of gold
          a gate of keep   a pound of flesh   a cent of rose
     a keep of out   a chain of links
a out of let   a rope of off   a stick of lip
          a myth of why   a knot of no
     a map of where   a hand of god   a back of up
          a guard of dog
a flag of state   a mob of rule   a fist of full
     a plot of land   a horde of food
          a thresh of hold
a pride of place   a field of force

time is of the essence

       no hour is too rushed in her small
city: by seven p.m. the traffic flows
       like liquid through a pipeline. she

stops at the corner station to fill
       up: the pump's familiar beeping sounds
consumer music. she points the nozzle,

       plunges it into her car, releases all she can
afford into its spacious depths. no
       rubber cup in place to capture excess

essence: so it ascends, dizzying, both
       fume and perfume, enters her body
like oxygen, drifts into her brain

       like the idea of waking. watching
the sun crash into a skyline cut flat
       where interstate 40 sweeps along

on stilts, she thinks about her honda's
       drink: what the paleozoic period
boiled down to. miles away, on

       the same planet, creatures of a new
era thunder around, care-less and
       cannibal in our desperate search

for fuel. she recaps her tank, fingers
       reeking. across the corner, the lot
at 1st street bar and grill is full. she

       knows the holocene will boil down, too,
someday: wonders how this crude age
       will have deposited anything of use.

writer's block

       she made connections, drew, created them—
or had they been there, waiting to be found?
       the rain went drop, drop, and a silver tomb
of ice encased each branch and limb. the ground

       whispered its wish, the limbs bent to hear, tried
to cry, the tears stuck fast. it broke them, fear
       they wouldn't see spring, and they didn't. sighed,
the slender trunks, into postures of prayer,

       and now they shoot their buds at her, like green
fires, sap barreling along, parallel
       to earth. the axes went chop, chop, to fell
the hangers-on that threatened overhead,

       the wood that would not. the will to (be) read
(is) (in) a splintered language, meant to mean.

ode to "e"

i am named for a poet who never in her lifetime
          published. her notebooks survive her—attic stacks
          of flimsy spiral-bound pads—narrow-ruled. her
poems read like grocery lists. *i need—a dozen eggs*
—a tub of lard—loaf bread—fatback—and rat poison
          for the rat who sleeps in my bed. hers is the poetics
          of the police log. 9/24/36—*his car was parked in front*
of her building last night—still there this morning—
this makes three nights straight. in a barely legible
          hand—she pens prescriptive lines. *i am sick*
          and tired of him. our boys ask questions—know better.
when he comes—he'll be drunk. i could use a drink
myself. her patterns weave a cover she leaves me—
          a cloak of many colors. i turn her legacy inside
          out and expose the seamy interior. what's in a
shame? o silent letters! o "e"s everywhere, with
all our cells of poetry—whatever worlds we're
          hiding from—whatever worlds we're hiding—

clutter

the wedding party occupied a bed & breakfast
                              near the lake,
in a neighborhood that had turned black
                    around its edges,
          as if the property were a cookie baked too fast,
                              at too high a temperature.
the owners,
          a slim unmemorable man   and a brown-
     haired woman who wore her cardigans
                    and birkenstocks with great   energy,
entertained lou and dee,
          captives on floral upholstery   in the dark living room,
while their husbands,   groomsmen,
                              rehearsed.
lou wondered,
     failing to focus on the earnest history
                    of the grand, old house,
          why *victorian* so often meant
                              cluttered.
had 19th century wealth   found its joy in saying,
                    i have several,
     when one *good* item   might have done?
dee nodded to the owners' drone.
                              lou counted
     one,   two,   three real or replica workboxes,
those kits in which ladies kept their sewing
          organized and handy,
     stationed here and there   about the room,
               one right beside the vcr.

when they were finally free to chat,
     lou and dee   sputtered   for the first minutes.
          oh, the travel...   ah, the wedding...

one subject clunking dully in the past,
           the other shimmering   just out of reach
                      in tomorrow.
well…their husbands?
     yes!   each loved the other's,
       properly, as wives of best friends ought.
each loved her own.   lou claimed she couldn't
       live without hers.
then, dry as powder,   dee drawled that hers was
     not the lighter in the matchbox
                 of her soul.
shocked, lou pressed for more.
      dee loved her husband like a christian,   she said,
          as her provider
       and the father of their someday children.
but excite her?   no,
     shaking her head-full of memories,
no passion like she'd had   for one or two men she loved
        back in her sinning days.
       is that enough,
lou wanted to know,   but she kept the question to herself,
             in the single workbox
     in the sitting room of her mind,
where she stored   all the questions she was
       working on,   like *is love enough?*
      a nettling one,   like a needlepoint in progress,
its soft white expanse stained
     with the delicate fragment of a scene,
with the needleworker's   careless blood.
     lou's workbox was cram-full of such questions.
       after that chat,
       lou thought of her friend as
dee-the-pragmatist,   and watched with   quizzing eyes
     when dee kissed her husband,
as if such lips   were lying.

the two women sat together at the wedding,
            witnessed one friend   marry another,
        smiled as their husbands offered arms   to bridesmaids.
*that trip down the aisle means   nothing   if
        you're not the bride,*   lou mused,
wistful but smug,   her jealousy mild,
                without the nasty flavor of insecurity.
        the reception,
            like a thick, colorful stew,
simmered on the bed & breakfast's wide,
                            wrap-around porch,
spilling onto the circular foyer's   marble floors
                        for dancing.
        the bride dropped her fistful of wilting flowers
                from halfway up the spiral staircase,
women clustered in the space   below,
            hoping to catch   the rosebud wedding bug.
lou and dee shared dinner conversation,   broken up
        by visits from their husbands,
                still on duty at the head table,
but unable to resist popping by from   time to time.
        lou's husband sipped water
                            from her sweating glass
            and nibbled bits of her chicken,
        as if   these spoils of marriage,
what's-yours-is-mine,   were better tasting than
            anything on his own plate.
        dee's husband was less flamboyant,   hovering
almost gratefully over his smiling wife.

dancing and champagne for everyone,   for hours,
        then the party deflated,   shrinking to nine or ten who'd
            be sleeping in the cluttered   rooms above.

lou's eyes followed the best man's solid form around the floor,
        as he waltzed solo   to *silly*, a song unique in
the evening's line-up,   r&b in 3/4 time.
        lou,   counting the steps,
wanting to learn,   to be whirled across marble
like a hoop-skirted   southern belle,   begged a lesson.
            but in his unfamiliar arms,
        under her husband's thick stare,
she was wooden,   even her smile unbending.
                    she suffered   through the dance,
        picturing dee's husband and   his pragmatic wife
already upstairs in bed,   comfortable
            in what they'd agreed to be
        to each other. lou prayed that she could satisfy herself,
                    from then on,
with learning   only what
        her husband's hands could teach her.
this new worry wouldn't fit   in her existing mental workbox,
            so she invented another,   recognizing,
                    with a sigh,
the irresistible beginnings of   clutter.

"at your age, he was preaching at the temple"

    just as i am
we sang, and i waded
through christians
to the front pew
trying not to grin
or frown, mimicking
imagined angels.
    without one plea
with one hand splayed
across the preacher's bible,
the other flat-palming
a promise: i confess. i am
one of you, the faithful,
the jesus-crazy.
    and waiting not
church ladies mother
me down the hall,
pat my shoulders fifty
blessèd times, drape white
cotton over a chair,
would undress me like
the newborn i will be.
    to rid my soul
a shower cap beneath
the loose hood, to save
my hair. a descent: a
blue-black submission:
    of one dark blot
faith into blood-
chilling waters. preacher's
hand in the small of
my back. i rise, streaming
sin, and doubt-dirty.
    just as i am

my last modernist poem, #2
(or, mugshot)

       don't say cover-up. this man's not masked,
he's the essence of out. the bare facts:
he's stripped his hair of naps, denuded
his skin, chiseled away the fleshy

       roundness of his face. his eyes remain
geometrically opposed to his
jaw. don't say cover-girl. no, he's a
harlequin without his diamond tear,

       mascaraed moats like tar encircling
his skewed view. ask yourself: who are his
models? liz or diana, maybe.
maybe he's reviving caesar or

       catullus, based on a bust, forced to
cast himself in blood, sweat, and marble.

blue-ing green: the sonobiography of miles davis

        blue flame the first thing he knew ::
st. louis blues with dizzying rules ::
        blue devil makes his pointed debut ::

blew into new york a westerly overture ::
        julliard dropout takes a bluebird tutor ::
blue demon seized by a gram reaper ::

        blooming of a green embouchure ::
blew and mellow in unmuted bell ::
        bills played in full circuitously ::
trane cruises through on steam heat ::

        thick green chords a sticky carpet ::
melodies return to aquamarine mood ::
        blue spring grew green a cash crop ::
ballads fuel a blown fuse future—

waiting for van gogh

the graveyard on the corner becomes the lower
jaw of a whale sown with crooked rows of
granite teeth. the roof of its mouth is the sky,
falling, the grassy dentured mounds struggle
up, the jaws of the whale close, and i am
outcast, neither ahab pursuing nor jonah
pursued, but woman, alone. *don't look at me!* i
will stone you from the heart out, a
postmodern medusa. *don't speak to me! stay with
me!* across the courtyard, a woman laughs as if
to remind me that mirth is a duty. i crush
headphones to my ears, close my eyes. i pass,
disembodied, into water in the key of c-minor,
where guitar licks are waves flicking salt onto
sand, bass riffs sound the green-black floor,
seaweed synthesizer runs undulate. immersed,
i'm alone, but for the gloomy impresario who
translates the wash of notes into a starry night.
sweet, single-eared rhythmist, with his
scratchy beard, straw hat, shiny trousers, and
high rear end. i like being alone with him. i can
be myself in his wild arms, like i can be myself
alone with you, here, in this white paper
epitaph, this tombstone poem.

disciple

my father: younger, handsome, downright square,
eyes like brown buttons fastening his face
over his soul, mouth not too straight to swear,
to say, *man, sonny stitt's ass trashed the place,*

hymning his saxophonist small-g god,
enlisted arms push-up strong, lips curled less
and less around cigarettes (in an odd
reversal of what the army did best:

march men to foul habits) and more around
his mouthpiece, in search of pure embouchure:
not square: hell-bent on welling a full sound
from his horn: a liquid literature

with biblical phrasing, an interlude
of stimulants unchemical to blood.

meditation: having everything to live for, the poet worries

a spring of undecided direction
        cool hot warm cool noons
my buttery belief in love's nonexistence   melting
my fluid faith in my body's   invincibility   fluttered
      by that old devil   western medicine
i am   in love and ill   at ease
the gardens so green
        alive with goslings   leaves   blooming lilacs
as if may came from here
and everywhere   i spy   metaphors for my condition
      because i am   conditioned to find them

the pond   cool and dark
              lidded with shadows of oaks
is the night-after-night of conversation
      i sink into   with a man   who's got
               big lungs   a strong heart
mornings   we surface like turtles   breathing in sleep
      sunlit sleep spent   redreaming our lunar-ruled exchanges

mallards occupy this water
      flocking from this bank   to the other
         pausing on the lawn to   beak at their sleek feathers
four or five relentless drakes
      chase one beleaguered duck   for hours   to mate mate mate
green-headed gallants hounding her brown body
      the way images   of white lab coats and sharps
        of slides and tiny tubes of legible blood
harry my   tired brain
maniacal honking   sounds
                     a haunting humor

knock my knuckles
       on the rain-washed wood of this bench
willing to placate fate   before
falling back on   the god of miracles
       to beg without ceasing   for well-being enough
to relish the blessing of   love
in return   o you   this poem
       the fabric of faith
wrapped around me   on display
       so long as late spring   afternoons
         threaten to be cool

ballad of bertie county

i.

it was our hope to get there long before
dark, but this part of carolina had been
dark for two hundred years or more:
dim-lit by white flames of cotton on thin

brown stalks. we were answering a call,
braving klan country to bring black folks
city words with rural roots. we were all
smiles with rough edges, telling bitter jokes.

ii.

sistah's house must be pretty big, we
joked, half-expecting to be bedded down
on cots and couches after eating all the
collard greens we could. the last town,

as sleepy as we were, some twenty, thirty
miles behind us now. we were gunning
our mouths, didn't hear the whispers we
should have heard. time's savage cunning.

iii.

around us, the trees silhouetted, blackened,
and disappeared into vast carolina night.
we chased our headlights. our pace slackened
when we spotted red-brick columns and white

picket fence. a gravel driveway led through
the columns towards a noose of yellow light
above a shuttered door. ancient pines grew
on either side, rising thickly, quickly out of sight.

iv.

not knowing what we'd gotten into, we
got out of the car. the land seemed to sigh,
a cricketless silence. we still didn't foresee
the plump white woman who greeted us. *hi,*

you must be…. come in. welcome. farewell,
welfare, we thought, and crossed the thresh-
hold. inside, one glance told us the deal. hell,
it really was a big house. memories in the flesh.

v.

no sign of mammy anywhere. no "wooly heads,"
no "pickaninnies," no grinning boy-men, in any
pictures, on any knick-knack shelves. our beds
in innocent, menacing rooms. how many, how many

slaved here? echoes of injuries rushing down
the spiral staircase at us, seeping from the wood
floor like sweat. none of us ever meant to drown
first-hand in such a flood. fate got us good.

vi.

burgundy candles burned, bleeding onto
the mahogany table. portraits of the mistress
and master, in silk and suit, hung like two
crimes on the opposite wall. our distress

crawled our skin like lice, as our hostess's aunt
and mother fished out story after story
from their wine glasses, dripping their debutante
drawls all over us, draping us in old glory.

vii.

we were never alone together, till she left
us for the night in our three unholy
rooms. gathering in one, we mourned the theft
of our choice, our right to claim, solely

for the sake of our historied hearts, *i* NEVER.
one of us drew a vial of oil from a pocket,
anointed our heads, hands, feet. *evil's clever.*
touch your windows and your door. and lock it.

viii.

there were forty-seven blacks enslaved here,
she'd told us. i sat up with all the lights
on till my eyelids dropped like tears. fear
dragged me through sleep, despite our rites.

i dreamed of forty-seven fiddles shrieking
dixie, forty-seven bales of cotton, forty-seven
hounds a-howling, forty-seven planters leaking
pus between brown thighs, and not one heaven.

ix.

morning. november's anemic sunlight swooned
across the yard and, beyond, the desolate field.
i sought sights to prove we weren't marooned
in 1850, 1940. watched an elder wearily wield

a rake, inherited work he'd spent a lifetime
doing, his payment a pittance little more than
slave wages. *historic preservation:* pastime
for mother and aunt, livelihood for this man.

x.

downstairs, in the kitchen, we sipped coffee,
waited on scrambled eggs. through a second
door, a room we hadn't seen last night. off we
went, drawing near the portrait that beckoned

us. *who's that? we asked. sis harriet, they
called her. harriet gatling. she was cook here, after
slavery.* so: *stand here,* said miss lady one day.
i want to paint you at…um…rest. laughter.

xi.

we breakfasted, packed, followed them
to the center to read our poems. exercise
equipment had been pushed to the gym
walls. *the only other place nearby of enough size*

for such a program is hope plantation, our hostess told
us. counting our blessings and our meager
but warm black audience, we let our words unfold
a map of farms and cities, migrations of the eager.

xii.

it was our hope to recover a newer world
before dark, but we had to drive across
centuries to get home. our directions wrong,
but our wills strong, we bore our mutual loss

in anything but silence, till we saw rocky mount
twinkling along the highway, a tight necklace
of lights. we swore to log this passage, to account
for this double-crossing, to etch an inerasable trace.

for lenard and teresa

notes for the early journey

somewhere along the way you will need to lean
over a bluff's edge   drop your shoes and keep moving   use
the feel of greening grass under your feet as a guide   if a
rainbow confuses you   which end   go the third
way   on the mountain you'll remember   climb on
up to where the aspens tremble   you will be alone   these
high winds can knife some lungs to gasping rags   but for you

there's nothing to worry about   breathe   sniff the air like
a bloodhound and head the opposite way   find the
place where the land dissolves into sand   keep walking   when
that sand becomes sea   speak a bridge into being
i know you can do it   your father's son ain't
heard of can't   follow the song   don't stop until you're south
of sorrow and all you can smell is jasmine   i never
once stumbled on such a place   hard to say if a brown child
in the last four hundred years has had such
a luscious dream   day or night   but this is your mother's
lullaby   i know she meant you to sleep sweet

for j.v.k.

iii. pull

– shall become as –

          you put this pen
in my hand and you
take the pen from
          my hand. the night
before the full moon

          the moon seems
full. what is missing
is a dark hungry
          sickle, the sliver
of shadow eating

          us up inside. after
the mountains breathe
their mint-and-sorrow
          green against the long
summer sky, they burst

          into hot october
laughter, lighting
the horizon with citrus,
          rust, and blood. you
put this knife in my

          hand. we pull. we
meet as oceans come
together, heaving
          against and clinging
across our salt watery

          boundary. we approach
endlessly like two rails
of one track, tied
          in a parallel that
promises our eyes to

merge, someplace far
off in the distance. you
put this feather in my
        palm. my fingers
close around flight.

in-trula (a poem for yellow mary's "traveling companion")

i. the journey

sweet butter-taffy siren: sand-colored
sophisticate: your wide, mute mouth, red-lipped,
hardened, like a candy-apple glaze:
your hazel eyes flashing laughter at
this *tu ne sais quoi* peazant nonsense:
beneath a cloud of honey n brown sugar hair,
whipped like cotton candy, you make merry:
a white silk parasol, your color-guard:
kaleidoscope mirrors flip you back your smile
and tender mary's grin spilt upside down:
how far we are from home you think but do
not say because you haven't been introduced

ii. the destination

what mirrors could truly reflect your constellation,
help them trace it in their midnight sky:
and how many tongues would have to come untied
for her to talk this island, these peazants,
into your blood and lungs the way you see
they filling yellow mary's: crisp white cotton
dresses skimming thick black boots: yards
of braided hair: ragged bags of roots:
a matriarch in indigo seals your fate:
there's no home for us here you think but do
not say cause mary done kissed that voodoo hand:
and wordless still you turn your back and fly

henry bibb considers love and livery

The circumstances of my courtship and marriage, I

       standing around   *flat-footed*   *love-grounded*

no wings no hope   *no fleet*   *vessel*   *vassal*

consider to be among the most remarkable events

star-struck   *seeing*   *dazed*   *stunned*

      standing around   *constellation*   *consolation*

of my life while a slave. To think that after I had

      via stars   *whiling*   *labored*   *willing*

to love   *head-first*   *head-over*   *heel*

determined to carry out the great idea which is so

bound   *bounded*   *headstrong*   *heady*

      transported   *exported*   *excess*

universally and practically acknowledged among all

      one good turn   *practice*   *perfect*

cosmos   *standing around*   *seeing*

the civilized nations of the earth, that I would be

citizen   *vessel*   *borne*   *vassal*

      gaea   *terra story*   *conditional*   *future perfect* free or die, I suffered myself to be turned aside

   to love   *bound*   *to mortify* *flesh*

liberty   *versus*   *one*   *star-struck*

   by the fascinating charms of a female, who gradually

spell   *bound*   *flesh*   *gaea*

   stellar   *light*   *years*   *slow burn*

won my attention from an object so high as that

   suffered   *labored*   *waiting* *rapt*

love-grounded   *standing around*   *stellar*

   of liberty; and an object which I held paramount

free   *flee*   *fleet*   *rapt*

   paramour *to love*   *manipulate* *via stars*

to all others.

   against stars

ballplayer

i cop a squat on a squared-off log,
to watch you ball on the community center court.
butt numb, i shift my weight

and shake mosquitos from my ankles,
but never take my eyes off the game.
yours follow the orange orb, your pupils
twin, brown moons reflecting its light.

your play is wild efficiency,
you are a four-pronged magic wand,
waving, as if agentless, in all directions at once.
an opponent dribbles the ball—now he sees it,

now he don't, it's gone, flown,
and you've given it its wings.
you are one-eighth of the shrieking rubber,

one-eighth of the growls and calls. you are
the delicious assist, the unerring pass.
you spread your skills out before me, a peacock
among pigeons, as if to say "all eyes on me,"

and make it worth my while.
a chill trails the sun west like a long, clammy train,
crawls over me and my makeshift bench,
over the emptying playground,

but stops at the edge of the concrete,
where eight men burning keep it at bay,
the way torches smoking around a patio

ward off insects. twilight rises like dark steam
from the dewy grass, but you don't see it.
the ball still lights the court
until the winning jumper sinks and puts it out.

then earth returns to view, and you jog over
to slap my palm and beam,
and receive the grin i give you like a trophy.

apples and oranges: *an allegory*

i was always an apple person, myself.
the variety! golden delicious,
the dark, deep red delicious, granny white, russet.
sweetsweetsweetsweet sweet sweet sweet!
bite in and let the juices commence to dribbling!

                                    oranges? if you've seen one orange,
                                        you've seen em all, i always said.
                                some of them have thicker skins than others,
                        but thick or thin, that white-orange rind has got to go
                                    before you get to anything you can use.
                                    i'd peeled a couple oranges in my day,
                                        just for the acid change of pace.
                                suck—pucker—not yucky, but too tart for me!

so i'm on the lookout for a good apple, okay,
a really good one,
a you-ain't-had-no-apple-like-this apple.

                                    and find myself with an orange.

now, it's not what you're thinking.
i had not searched high and low for a good apple.
i had not been around the world trying to find a good apple.
i had not given up all hope of ever putting my hands
on a good apple.
some of my friends had damn good apples,
and i knew where they got em
and i knew there were more where those came from.
i was figuring i'd stumble upon a good apple any minute.

                                          so when i pick up this orange
                                    i'm not just dying for any ole fruit.
                                        but it's there, round and bright,
                             and when i squeeze it, i can feel the juices
                                              just beneath the surface.
                                   i figure i'll peel it—what the hell!
                                              maybe it'll be sweet,
                          one of those rare honey-sunshine oranges,
                                      and i'll be glad i took the time.

                                            it is a damn good orange.
                             the kind of orange you have to take slow,
                                                 section by section.
                                       i'm still working on that orange.

now, it's not what you're thinking.
i'm still an apple person, myself.
an apple person who knows that

                                            all oranges are not alike.
                                                      there's some

like apples.

daddy's girl

you call. i take your raspy *hey, baby*
like a vaccine. your approach is back-door,
attuned to years of piss-poor welcome.

we are both helpless in the groove: you
mirror me my splotchy humanity, when i'm
going for goddess, demanding worship

from the apogee, like a nappy-headed
diana. back off. come back. when i was four,
i planned to marry you, with bright penny-

certainty. who else? told mommy so. (freud,
kiss my ass.) of *course* you pick pestalozzi, some
swiss guy with ideas about kindergarten,

for your philosopher-hero. your students,
brown-faced september daisies, sprout annually
for thirteen years, always freshly five and

asking for nothing more than an alphabet.
but daughters are perennial. like trees, we grow
up and up, thicken, spread out. sure, we

shed our trimmings, start again, but never
from scratch. at twenty-six, i write myself madly
out of your grasp, running smack into a ted

hughes of my own. at the wedding, i am white
and stiff as a taper. you are smiling like a convict.
i take the petal-strewn paper-carpet stroll

alone, like a good feminist. your face is joy
in watercolors, right on the verge of becoming
something else. damn it, the *one* time

it isn't personal, you get hurt. i register
the frost in your moustache, the blizzard blotting
your mental landmarks, and growl. april

is cruel, but december's only humoring us.
i am the sun, caged in a ptolemaic nightmare. no,
i am galileo facing a ritual inquisition: *be*

a sweet girl for daddy, okay? i spit out
heliocentric heresies: i am thirty-three and my
moves are measured in galaxies, not days!

now what? you gonna cut out my tongue,
wash my fucking mouth out with soap? *don't*
talk that way to me. i'm still your father.

i grip the receiver like a steering wheel.
rub my red eyes. squint into the distance
lowered between us like a shade. if

you were the vast pacific and i, pushed
from a raft just cresting the navel of your muddy
belly, i still couldn't fall into your arms.

you must walk this lonesome

say hello to moon leads you into trees as thick as folk on easter pews dark but venture through amazing was blind but now fireflies glittering dangling from evergreens like christmas oracles soon you meet the riverbank down by the riverside water bapteases your feet moon bursts back in low yellow swing low sweet chariot of cheese shines on in the river cup hands and sip what never saw inside a peace be still mix in your tears moon distills distress like yours so nobody knows the trouble it causes pull up a log and sit until your empty is full your straight is wool your death is yule moonshine will do that barter with you what you got for what you need draw from the river like it is well with my soul o moon you croon and home you go

double bop for ntozake shange

waiting, we paced the cages of our desires,
the stage a big yellow maw, toothless, unable
to snag you. we stalked you with our voices,
invoked your name with the rough insistency
of the sea calling the earth with its long
wet tongue. where (where) could you be?

why you wanna treat me so bad,
when you know i love you?

were you absent like the moon: not gone,
but hidden in the shadow of a mood?
were you buried like a maple in a january
silence? voodoo priestess, off tracking
word-herbs to their lairs in dark woods,
you kept us waiting, sprawled across
the rigid network of seats like so much
spanish moss, a fungus of patience.

why you wanna treat me so bad

arriving, you staggered, no, tightroped
your way to the mic. your hollow apology
rang with the purity of a spoon tapped
against plastic. reading, your words poured
like oatmeal, clumped and milky, over your
red lips. what could (be) wrong (with) you?

why you wanna treat me so bad

where have you been that wouldn't
let you go? and what fist of gas, what
explosion of tubed or bottled liquid,
have you wombed, to replace what was
ripped away from you in your leaving?

negra salsera, dancing to the erratic
beat of a different congo, you read
the dim corners of our illegible minds.

why you wanna treat me so bad

meeting, you and we spat in each other's
faces. swaying into the mic, you sang (to)
your absent ripped-away part. we shared
our shame in humid sighs that circulated
like clotting blood through thickened
veins, but we couldn't leave you (be).

you know i love you?

you remind me

of a liquid-eyed lover i loved
torrentially, 3 springs ago: same
laughter gurgling in the throat, rushing
over tongue and teeth like white water
rapids toward a falls: same scent, jasmine
and rain, in your skin: same narrow hips
disappearing into short, stocky
thighs: so like her, another plain, brown
paper package concealing a spill
of diamonds and rubies glittering
as if wet / a golden pastry baked
around apple slices / explosives /
a white lace teddy, virginal and
open at the crotch: *yes:* but when i
touch you there, you release a music
all your own: violet melody,
walking blue bass: a jazz riff, scaling
the black keys, winging away from the
standard that spawned it: *your* low-pitched
croon creates this nipple-thrill, calls
my lips to your moist belly: you are
the phoenix, the medusa, the moon:
i know you by the melted-butter
consistency of your cream, the rough
curl of your thatch of hair, the power
of your luscious muscles contracting
warm around my searching fingers

back in a minute

he arrived at her station like the night
train, right on time yet unexpected, scarfless
and casual, belying the distance traveled,

cargo cowering in the boxcar he'd have sworn
he'd left behind. she dispensed him gasoline
and cigarettes, safely encased in pock-marked

bullet-proof plastic, draped in a blue
smock, *lilene* embroidered above her right
breast. *you look like a mother,* he muttered

around the brown filter, through white smoke
and yellow teeth. *how old is your son?*
eighteen months, she replied, and in the same

thin tone charged him *eighteen fifty-three*
for his fuel. good, he said. *i haven't missed much.*
she squinted at him, peering between bars

of mascara. she found his depth a tree-studded
whiteness, dirt entombed beneath snow. *you*
look like a song, she chanted, her voice filtering

through the rigid clear plastic mesh, *one*
about a man who drove across three state lines
to find cigs. he filled his lungs with her

words, but couldn't hold them. she watched
as the truth seeped out, puddled in
the space beneath his nostrils like a cloud,

and disappeared as quickly as it could. *when
do you get off?* he asked, his question
the sound of a hand held out for change. *i'll*

wait for you. she shook her head, with its
impoverished clutch of hair, thinking *where
do you get off?*, reading him like a bedtime

story. *go home,* she said and did not say,
*the woman you think i am is waiting for
you. go home, if it takes you all damn night.*

poem *for when his arms open* *so wide* *you fall through*

a disappointment — a devastation — a disaster — a deviation
all of the above — at least
(at best)

requires the loss — and that is what — the first / and the last — but perhaps the gift / i am waiting to see / wrapped so nicely / in the tree
i am testing trust — going out on a limb / that just dropped me — shake the ticking package

right / in my soul — a word-worker / in letters of blood / whose blood — because one bad branch / don't spoil the whole trunk — has inscribed his name
and the question is — or how many people's

is it still bleeding / or simply a red record of — what bled — when did it all / get so complicated — so many complications

love — and here i was thinking — that love is just — i thought it was just

trust

aftermath

the beginning. after all, when she

knife. the way summer or spring

couldn't have missed. and the many-

his leg always shook like that, now

of the world was supposed to swirl

and shot. stock optioned and

giggling for days. in long final

over. you could have done the math

the aftermath is always there from

kissed you, the butter slid off your

followed winter was a sign you

eyed potatoes, you didn't believe

did you? *did you?* water this part

the other direction. arrows pointed

dropped. a funny smell had you

division, something's always left

before.

lifeline

wedged in the top branches, rain still sighing
          to earth as a dissolute sky dissolves,
a mozambican woman turns mother,
          her water breaking loose to pool with the flood

licking the trunk below. a country-sized
          puddle calls forth the child whose name, the mother
vowed, would not be *drowned*, no matter how
          high she had to climb. my mother's water

washed her bare yellow bathroom tile many
          years ago, a diluvial warning
of my struggle to arrive. we fought to
          get me out, and have been tugging at each

other ever since, tethered by a cord
          that simply thickens when it's cut. we
descended then, thirsting, churning, not into
          the waters that hound the mozambican

mother, baying her and her baby in
          the tree, but into that enduring ocean
in which—as mother, daughter, or both—a
          woman's only choices are drink or swim.

hartwell dam

i wondered if effortless lives were the inherent
        property of whiteness, wondered if i might
marry into it, the expectation of a life of days
        like today, a birthday celebrated in cool shade
and blond sunshine, beneath and beside two
        of the bluest blues that georgia could produce,
as atmosphere and lake vied for bragging rights,
        a bottle of wine chinking solidly against the rough
stone of the table after each tour of our plastic
        cups, the last slice of pizza releasing its last
heat, the air whispering through the thin stack
        of napkins, exsiccating any chance of sweat, as
if to say *at your service,*

                        though even as i let
        myself imagine privilege as a sort of genetic
trait, i imagined my favorite harlem renaissance
        figures in picturesque settings or elegance, once
upon a time, du bois and fauset in white gloves,
        white pearls, with the handles of ivory teacups
in their careful, almost-entitled fingers, lightly
        held, or tightly, with digit-numbing control, like
me, perhaps, a little chilled, from apprehension
        as much as my breeze or their too-conditioned
air, the tiny goose-bump-inducing fear that we
        may be asked to leave, politely or not, id'd
by dna as uninvited and escorted to the door
        by unapologetic maitre d's,

                                or in my case, more
likely shouted back to africa by confederate-flag-
        waving rabid young men with red faces, passing
by our little spread on the way to their pickups,
        squaring the round face of the mother across from

me, whose rejection could freeze me cold, far
        more than any rebel's, whose own presence here
might've elicited a spit-out wish that she go home
        to france, if nationality were visible from a stone's
throw away, whose son, with his two-homes-or-
        none-at-all transatlantic blues, is the man for
whom i've fallen like a swooning southern belle
        in blackface,

                        making her, the happy birthday girl,
the woman who could make my life hell, if she
        wanted, drawing my gratitude for what should be
par for the course, my inclusion in this intimate
        family lunch, the teasing and confidences, straight-
forward questions and good-humored acceptance
        of my eccentricities, my determination to plant
myself in a nearby swing and pump my brown legs
        into the more distant blue, while they dregged
the wine,

        which left her sated and comfortable
        enough to stretch out on the bench, even able
to nap, where i never could, her arm above her
        head, with nothing but the autumn sun for cover,
while her son and i tramped the embankment
        together, holding each other as if we were meant
for it, trying and trying not to disregard what
        we've inherited—skin, hair, culture—not to shut
some door we can't reopen, stumbling through
        the sunlit darkness toward whatever love can do,
returning to lure his mother from her feral sleep,
        hoping, each of us, that such strange days would keep.

                for aline

á table

they love him and i was with him:
        so they passed me the baguette,
to rip off a fist-sized chunk, golden

crust flaking onto the tablecloth
        in a crisp snow: they served up
salmon, smoked, with dill sauce,

thin slices of color itself: they
        tossed simple salads, lettuce
and oil, and stuffed tomatoes

for us, the vegetarian they love
        and the woman he loves: they
put out plates of cheese, insisted

i try a bit of *chevre* so strong it could
        have lifted the goat it came from:
they initiated me into the art

of the *apértif,* cassis, just so much,
        and chardonnay, electric currants
in a glass: they knew we could not

have food like this *aux états-unis,*
        melon as delightful as a silk
blouse against the shoulders, no,

wine as full and textured as sex,
        not possible, not to be believed
of the land of pagan cuisine: they

demanded, every uncle, aunt,
        and cousin, that we open our mouths,
throw back our heads, and swallow

all the family they could fit into one
        two-week visit: they hosted lunches
that lasted from noon to nine, dinners

that kept us feasting till we could
        neither sit nor stand: they produced
omelettes that rose above the pan's

edge like sunrise: they emptied
        their kitchens into our sated stomachs,
and when we were staggering under

a half-dozen courses, they presented
        the irresistibles, the *tartes* topped
with beautiful fruit, the chocolate

gateaux, the *flans,* and floating islands
        of meringue that some or all of us
must have dreamed up: they loved

us with rich, black coffee sweetened
        with honey from their hives: they
taught me their tongue: their toasts,

their jokes, their silences, their loud
        beliefs and quiet griefs, all the things
they bring to their tables: they taught me

how to be a part of them, who are a
        part of him, and i am replete with
kith and kin: i am gourmet, *gourmande.*

                aux ménétriers et robolins

a course in canvas

glasper casts an agile shadow : : *left hand step to right hand float* : : runagate
pace, *pace* the forgetful : : *left hand do what right hand do* : : playing the changes
a century don't make : : *left hand shade while right hand color* : : pulls the 90s
up at the roots : : *left hand cradle the right hand blue-bop* : : transplants the tuber
into tyner's soil : : *left hand respond to right hand call* : : hip hop head all locks
and keys : : *left hand swing and right hand scatter* : : timely, composed in shifty
signatures : : *left hand throw what right hand blueing* : : glasper's a hobo riding
the rail : : *left hand steal away right hand home*

notes

Epigraphs: Wheatley's letter appears in *The Collected Works of Phillis Wheatley* (ed. John Shields), in the Schomburg Library of Nineteenth-Century Black Women Writers series (Oxford University Press, 1988). Lucille Clifton's lines are from "if something should happen," published in *Good Woman: Poems and a Memoir, 1969–1980* (BOA Editions, 1987).

p. 2: "london bridge" is one of three acrostic poems in this collection; the others are "you can say that again, billie" and "notes for the early journey."

p. 4: "pantoum: landing, 1976" was written with apologies and thanks to George Clinton and Julie Dash.

p. 5: "waiting on the mayflower" is based on dates taken from Lerone Bennett, Jr.'s book *Before the Mayflower: A History of Black America* (Penguin, 6th Reprint ed. 1993): August 1619—first Africans on North American soil; December 1638—first slaveship in the Bay State harbor; and March 1770—first martyr to the American Revolution.

p. 10: "o pioneer!" honors three African American men who all were made partners in one of Chicago's largest law firms in the same year, 1998—an unprecedented event among major law firms nationwide.

p. 12: "castillo del morro" takes its name from the fort in Old San Juan, Puerto Rico and translates roughly as "Castle on the Bluff."

p. 16: "the last temptation: a 21st-century bop odyssey" contains italicized lines which are lyrics from a recording by The Temptations.

p. 27: "you can say that again, billie" references Thomas Sutpen, a character in William Faulkner's novel *Absalom! Absalom!* (Vintage, 1991) who repudiates his wife and their son when he learns they have "Negro blood."

p. 30: "protect yourself" is written after André Fougeron's painting *Civilisation Atlantique.*

p. 40: "blue-ing green: the sonobiography of miles davis" references moments and people described in *Miles: The Autobiography* (Simon & Schuster, 1989).

p. 41: "waiting for van gogh" includes italicized lines from Samuel Beckett's work.

p. 45: "ballad of bertie county" was originally published with companion poems by Lenard D. Moore and L. Teresa Church.

p. 55: "in-trula" follows Yellow Mary Peazant and Trula, characters in Julie Dash's film *Daughters of the Dust,* as they journey together to the Sea Islands.

p. 56: "henry bibb considers love and livery" takes its unitalicized lines from the opening of Chapter III of the *Narrative of the Life and Adventures of Henry Bibb, An American Slave, Written By Himself* (University of Wisconsin Press, 2000).

p. 65: "double bop for ntozake shange" incorporates, as italicized lines, lyrics from Prince's song "Why You Wanna Treat Me So Bad?" (*Prince,* Warner, 1979).

acknowledgements

I would like to thank the editors of the journals, anthologies, and other publications in which poems in this collection have appeared:

Some poems were or will be published in the following print and online forums: *African American Literature and Culture Society Newsletter* ("a thousand words"); *African American Review* ("ballad of bertie county"); *Asheville Poetry Review* ("lifeline"); *Beloit Poetry Journal* ("possibilities of poetry, upon her death," "hartwell dam," and "notes for the early journey"); *Blink* ("bio/*autography* [or, 18th-century multiculturalism]"); *Blue Mesa Review* ("you remind me"); *BMa: The Sonia Sanchez Literary Review* ("in trula [a poem for yellow mary's 'traveling companion']"); *Brilliant Corners* ("disciple"); *The Café Review* ("waiting for van gogh"); *Callaloo* ("the ballad of anita hill"); *Crab Orchard Review* ("ballplayer"); *Drumvoices Revue* ("pantoum: landing, 1976"); *Fascicle* ("a thousand words"); *Hambone* ("back in a minute," "not in the causal chain," and "london bridge"); *HOW2* ("meditation: having everything to live for, the poet worries," "you can say that again, billie," and "poem   for when his arms open   so wide   you fall through"); *Legal Studies Forum* ("lifeline," "the ballad of anita hill," "you must walk this lonesome," and "o pioneer!"); *Melic Review* ("disciple"); *MiPOesias* ("elocation [or, exit us]"); *Mixed Blood* ("henry bibb considers love and livery," "atlantis made easy," and "unbelievable sale!"), *The News & Observer* ("time is of the essence"); *nearSouth* ("blue-ing green: the sonobiography of miles davis"); *Obsidian III* ("waiting on the mayflower," "double bop for ntozake shange," and "daddy's girl"); *nocturnes (re)view* ("castillo del morro: calling your bluff," "you can say that again, billie," and "ode to 'e'"); *Poetry Daily* ("bio/*autography* [or, 18th-century multiculturalism]"), and *Titanic Operas* ("writer's block," "protect yourself," and "o pioneer!").

Some are anthologized in: *Rainbow Darkness: An Anthology of African American Poetry* ("my last modernist poem, #2 [or, mugshot]);" "– shall become as – ," and "cause i'm from dixie too"); *Cave Canem III: 1998 Anthology* ("'at your age, he was preaching at the temple'"); *The Lucifer Poetics Group Displayer: Volume One* ("o pioneer!"); *Poetry 180: A Turning Back to Poetry* ("ballplayer"); and *Poetry Daily: Poems from the World's Most Popular Poetry Website* ("bio/*autography* [or, 18th-century multiculturalism]").

"the ballad of anita hill," "daddy's girl," "double bop for ntozake shange," "you remind me," "you must walk this lonesome," and "in-trula: (a poem for yellow mary's 'traveling companion')" appeared previously in my chapbook, *The Gorgon Goddess* (Carolina Wren Press, 2001).

"lifeline," "london bridge," "notes for the early journey," "you can say that again, billie," "apples and oranges: an allegory," "á table," and "ballad of bertie county" are accessible on the website *From the Fishouse: An Audio Archive of Emerging Poets.*

I would also like to thank the Hedgebrook Retreat Center for Women Writers for a two-week residency in 2003, during which some of these poems were intially written.

Finally, it is my pleasure to thank publicly two dear poet-friends who entered my life as incredible teachers of poetry, George Elliott Clarke and Lucille Clifton, along with the writing communities that have been most important to my work over the last ten years: the Carolina African American Writers Collective, which welcomed me into the North Carolina writing scene in 1996; the "Volls" (my housemates at Squaw Valley Community of Writers Poetry Workshop in 1999), who kept up a vibrant email correspondence for three or four years after our week together; the 4-Bean Stew poetry collective (especially Mendi Lewis Obadike and Christian Campbell), by whatever name we may call ourselves; the North Carolina poets who gathered periodically under the Lucifer Poetics Group moniker during the last couple of years before I moved to New Jersey; and the faculty and fellows of Cave Canem (especially those from 1997–99), without whom I would not be the poet I am today. To you all, my deepest gratitude.

The cover art for this book is "Red Sea"
© 2004 Maria Entis.
The text of the book is typeset in 10-point Minion.
The book was designed by Lesley Landis Designs
and printed by Central Plains Book Manufacturing.